DRAWN OUT *for a* PURPOSE

ISBN: 978-1-7350897-0-6

For ordering information please visit the author's website at www.pastorcisco.com or email us at pastorcisco924@gmail.com

First printing addition 2020

Printed in the United States of America

DRAWN OUT *for a* PURPOSE

Discovering God's Divine Purpose for Your Life

SAMUEL DUNCAN, IV

CONTENTS

ACKNOWLEDGEMENTS

T o all my family and friends that have supported me from day one; whether you entertained my big dreams and monsterous ideas, spoke kind words (and sometimes words of correction, rebuke, and reprove), or encouraged me when times were tough; I appreciate you more than words will allow me to express.

FOREWORD

There is great tragedy in loss, but a greater tragedy in living without a sense of purpose. For a little more than three decades, I have stood before thousands and facilitated hundreds of sessions filled with people who all share one common quest. That common quest is to discover and fulfill their purpose. I am elated to provide a foreword for this book. The content aligns with my personal values and philosophically pairs well with many of the greats in our field. This book has the same paroxysm as books by author-speakers including; Les Brown, Eric Thomas, Anthony Robbins, Jim Rohn, DeVon Franklin, and others on the subject. Samuel Duncan IV, as these best-selling motivators, inspires readers to maximize their lives through the discovery and pursuit of purpose. Ecclesiastes 3 tells us: "There is a time and a season to every purpose under the heavens." The Book of Wisdom then begins to itemize situations that afford us the opportunity to find balance in both victories and what looks like insurmountable challenges. The sum total of the seasons is identified as times in our lives that we face the opportunity to manifest purpose. I believe purposes are introduced by God's unmistakable plan. In other words, there is a plan for every living soul that has the potential to become everything that God has intended. It has been my experience after serving in ministry and facilitating professional development training for 35 years, was that people live with the question of "what is my purpose? ". While this question is not an indictment, it can, however, lead to a guilty verdict. Many people, both in and outside of the body of Christ are guilty of presuming that they will never know why they were created. This book helps to answer questions and also offers insightful strategies on discovering, embracing, and manifesting purpose. A central theme in the lives of successful people is understanding God's intended purpose for their lives. The pursuit of this purpose becomes the preoccupation of those who answer life's call. Specifically, when you identify your purpose, every day becomes an intentional journey to accomplish your God-given potential. I believe that goals and objectives become drivers toward the destiny that God maps out for every person. It is our task to pursue the journey with passion. This book offers an insightful look at purpose from a practitioner's perspective. Samuel Duncan IV has cultivated a diamond mine of priceless value in the following pages. I have known him to preach and practice all of the principles he captures in this great resource. Because he possesses both the academic and practical knowledge about the pursuit of purpose, these words of wisdom touch on biblical and present-day truths. As a key-member of the Strategic Growth and Development Team for the Michigan Southwest Third Ecclesiastical Jurisdiction of the Church of God in Christ, Samuel Duncan IV (also affectionately known as Pastor C), specializes in bringing simplicity to significance. Both in the areas of leadership development and fiscal governance, he uses almost 20 years of experience to help people find and fulfill their purpose in ministry and business environments. Pastor C brings clarity to why the pursuit of purpose is vital. He challenges readers with the perspective of being "Drawn Out for A Purpose". Enjoy!

Pastor Tarence E. Lauchiè

INTRODUCTION

D o you ever wonder about life? Have you ever pondered one or more of these questions – "Who am I? Why am I on Earth? Why was I created by God? What do I want to do with my life?"

These thoughts run through our minds occasionally. Waking up every day full of unanswered questions and nothing to look forward to achieving during the day, can be frustrating. It is worse when it seems like everyone around you is doing something worthwhile, fulfilling purpose in some way while you are unable to make sense of the direction your life is headed. Perhaps you grew up hearing about the great plans God has in store for you. However, you still struggle to reconcile His promises with your reality. You are at the stage of your life where you need clarity and direction so you can make better choices. Maybe you have had negative experiences, some caused by poor choices you made in the past. So, like Nathaniel's words when he heard about the Messiah from Nazareth, you wonder if anything good can come out of your life.

If this is you, I wrote this book as a special gift to you. We are all here on Earth for a length of time – a mystery known only to God. What this means is that you can not tell the hour nor the day you will leave this Earth. It is just like James said,

> James 4:14 "How do you know what your life will be like tomorrow? Your life is like the morning fog—it's here a little while, then it's gone." [NLT].

Time has been given to us as a gift to discover God's divine purpose for our lives and work hard at fulfilling it. In the end, the worth of our lives will be measured by how well we maximized our time here on Earth, carrying out God's divine purposes. For this reason, we must understand the meaning of our existence. Many have walked and exited this Earth, unable to find meaning for their existence. They died, ignorant of God's divine purpose for their lives, never realizing or maximizing their full potential. Les Brown once said,

"The graveyard is the richest place on earth because it is there that you will find all the hopes and dreams that were never fulfilled, the books that were never written, the songs that were never sung, the inventions that were never shared, the cures that were never discovered, all because someone was too afraid to take that first step, keep with the problem, or determined to carry out their dream."

Discovering God's divine purpose for your life - the reason for your existence is one of the most important secrets of a fulfilled life. On several occasions in the Holy Scriptures, men and women discovered God's divine purpose for their lives, dared to believe it, and rose to become relevant voices and changemakers in their generation. Despite their negative past experiences, God did not change their minds about them. Rather, He allowed them to choose to embrace His will for their lives. Although most of them had rough starts, their obedience to God's call on their lives, elevated them and glorified the Father.

Moses, for instance, was a child born in perilous times. Pharaoh had just declared the drowning of every newborn Hebrew male. However, God had a plan for His life. Moses, as his name signifies, was drawn out from the water for a specific purpose - to deliver the Israelites from captivity and lead them to the land God promised Abraham. He caused Moses to find favor in the eyes of Pharaoh's daughter. She adopted him as her son. However, several years down the line, he couldn't withstand the way his people were being mistreated. He tried in his way to protect his people by killing an Egyptian taskmaster, an act that cost him his position at the Palace. So, Moses, a murderer, fled Egypt and stayed in Midian for 40 years where he settled for a normal life as a shepherd, a husband, and a father. While Moses' situation looked bad to himself and others, God used those experiences to prepare him for his assignment. Responding to God's call transformed him from a murderer to a fierce warrior, leader, and deliverer of the Israelites.

Paul, another example of a man drawn out of his wicked ways to fulfill God's divine purpose. For many years, he persecuted the church and killed many saints. However, God preserved him. God, in all of His power, could have ended Paul's life instantly but he did not.

While others saw Paul as a murderer, persecuting the Christians, God saw him as the minister who would bring the message of salvation to the gentiles. Joseph, a young boy hated by his brothers for being a dreamer, was condemned in a pit. His brothers considered him a threat and decided to end his life. God ensured Joseph was preserved for a divine purpose. From being a faithful slave, imprisoned for a crime he did not commit; He was appointed prime minister. That position saved the sons of Israel from being victims of famine. His divine purpose was to preserve the generation from which Jesus descended.

I can go on and on giving examples of men and women who responded to the call of God for their lives. Their lives were transformed significantly. Some were on the verge of death. Some were rejected and considered as unworthy. Some made grievous mistakes. Yet, God preserved them for His divine purpose. Despite the challenges you have encountered in life, God has a divine purpose for your life. You are not a mistake. You were created for a specific reason. You were drawn out of sin and redeemed by Christ so you can discover and fulfill your assignment here on Earth. God was already prepared for your arrival to this earth in advance. He is not so much concerned with how you got here. Rather,

He is more interested in using you as a vessel to display His glory in the earth through who and what He has called you to be and do - His divine purpose for you!

I wrote this book as a guide to help believers, including you, dear friend, discover and fulfill the divine purpose in which God intends. I will be using real-life examples to help you understand the concept of divine purpose practically. Through the content in this book, you will learn about God's purpose for your life. Your past does not in any way define you. It does not affect God's purpose for your life. The simple yet life-transforming principles I will be sharing in this book will help you live intentionally, focused on fulfilling God's will for your life. I desire that as you read this book, may the Lord grant you an understanding of how you can apply these principles to transform your life. Remember, you are not a mistake. God created you for a divine purpose. Together, we will discover this unique purpose so you can live a life that pleases God - a fulfilled life.

CHAPTER 1

WHAT IS DIVINE PURPOSE?

Psalms 139:16 *"Your eyes saw my unformed body; all the days ordained for me were written in your book before one of them came to be.* **[NIV].**

The greatest tragedy in life is not death, but a life without a purpose.

—Dr. Myles Munroe

What comes to mind when you hear the word "Purpose?"

Purpose is the reason why a being was created or a thing exists. It answers the question, "Why am I here?" It is the intention behind the manufacturer's decision to create that product. For instance, a pressing iron was made for straightening our clothes so that we can look smart and beautiful in public. Without a pressing iron, you might be forced to come to work or attend an event with rumpled clothes. For example, say someone decides to use the pressing iron to toast bread, which would be considered an abuse of purpose. Why? That is because the manufacturer intended for the product to be used to enhance our appearance, not cooking our meals. For this reason, every product comes with a manual that helps the owner understand the purpose of the product and how they can use the product effectively.

Do you know your purpose, the reason why you were created? What is God's divine purpose for your life? In this chapter, we will be examining God's original intention for creating you and how you can discover your role in His divine purpose.

Understanding God's divine purpose for your life

Dr. Myles Munroe of blessed memory once said that "when the purpose of a thing is unknown, abuse is inevitable". When you do not know who you are and why you exist, you will expend time, energy, and resources doing the opposite of the will of God for your life.

God's divine purpose for your life is simply His reason for creating you, endowing you with the special abilities you have, and strategically placing you here on Earth. Like we said earlier, no manufacturer creates anything without a reason. Following the pressing iron illustration above, it is obvious that you are not a mistake. There is a reason God created you and placed you in your mother's womb. There is a reason for your family background, skin color, height, and everything else about you. There is also a reason for the experiences you have had, both positive and negative. They are clues and pointers to who you are and your reason for existence. So, despite all you have been told in the past about yourself, I want you to know that God did not make a mistake creating any part of you. Every part of your being is carefully knitted together to help you discover and fulfill God's divine purpose for your life.

Now, you might be wondering, "What is God's Divine Purpose for my life? How do I know the exact reason I was created?" That's why I am writing to help you understand His divine purpose so that you can make informed choices starting today. God's manual for mankind is the Bible. Through His Holy Spirit, He inspired people to compile the scriptures for doctrine, correction, reproof, and instruction in righteousness.[1] To understand why you were created, we have to go back to the beginning. After creating the Heaven and the Earth, filling the Earth with things he considered good, the following ensued;

> Genesis 1:26-27 Then God said, "Let Us make man in Our image, according to Our likeness; **let them have dominion over the fish of the sea, over the birds of the air, and the cattle, over all the earth and over every creeping thing that creeps on the earth.**" So, God created man in His image; in the image of God He created him; male and female He created them. Then God blessed them, and God said to them, "**Be fruitful and multiply; fill the earth and subdue it; have dominion over the fish of the sea, over the birds of**

---

[1] https://www.biblegateway.com/passage/?search=2+Timothy+3%3A16-17&version=NKJV

the air, and over every living thing that moves on the earth." [NKJV].

Notice the bolded parts of that scripture. The first part highlights God's original intention for creating us. He created us to have dominion over everything He created on the Earth. This means that your primary assignment here on Earth is to rule over everything he created, all except human beings. The word "Dominion" is derived from the root word "Radah". Radah means "to rule, have dominion, dominate, tread down." It also means to have complete authority over something. God who is eternal in His purpose, created us to rule over the Earth. That was our first assignment. He put us in charge as a king of this domain, the Earth. We were made to dominate the Earth using our God-given abilities, and the vast resources on the Earth to serve God and humanity.

After creation, he blessed man (male and female) and gave specific instructions on how they can dominate the Earth. He gave blessings before the instructions because you cannot fulfill God's divine purpose without His blessings upon your life. You cannot perform beyond His ability in you. The blessings empower you to carry out His instructions. It's just like Paul said,

Philippians 2:13 "For it is God who works in you both to will and to do for His good pleasure." [NKJV].

So, God's Divine Purpose for our creation was Dominion of the Earth and everything in it. He made us just like Him so that we can effectively carry out this assignment, bringing glory to His name. Although this was God's original intention, man's disobedience of God's instructions led to a loss of his dominion over the Earth. He also lost communion with God. He lost the ability to enjoy fellowship with God and build intimacy with Him. Because we all descended from Adam, we partook of the consequences of his disobedience.[2] To restore Man to His original intention for creation, God sent His son Jesus Christ to pay the ultimate price for our redemption. Jesus came to Earth to do the following;

- Restore our communion with God;
- Restore us to His image;
- Restore Dominion over the domain (Earth) He gave us complete authority over.

---

[2] https://www.biblegateway.com/passage/?search=1%20Corinthians%2015:22&version=NLT

So, the reason you did not go to heaven after Salvation is because you have work to do. God restored you to carry out the assignment He predestined for you. Paul's letter to the Church in Ephesus, expressly states the reason for our redemption. He said,

> Ephesians 2:10 "For we are God's [own] handiwork (His workmanship), recreated in Christ Jesus, [born anew] that we may do those good works which God predestined (planned) for us [taking paths which He prepared ahead of time], that we should walk in them [living the good life which He prearranged and made ready for us to live]." [AMPC].

God saved mankind to fulfill His divine purpose on the Earth. You were recreated in Christ Jesus to fulfill God's desire in a given place and season. Recreated simply means that as a result of Jesus' ultimate sacrifice, you have a chance to do the work that God has pre-crafted you for. That is why Jesus re-emphasized God's purpose for our lives in the book of Matthew. He said in Matthew 5:16, "Let your light so shine before men, that they may see your good works and glorify your Father in heaven." [NKJV].

Identifying your role in God's divine purpose

Having understood that God's divine purpose for us is to dominate the Earth, using our abilities and vast resources on the Earth to achieve this purpose, you must discover your role in His agenda. One of the questions you must ask yourself is this "what good works did God predestine me to complete on this Earth? What is my role in His Dominion Mandate?" Everyone has a unique role to play in fulfilling His eternal purpose because we are wired differently. Just like different parts of the body have individual roles but together, they carry out one purpose. We all have unique strengths and abilities that make our assignment differ from that of others.

Sometimes, we fall to the temptation of comparing ourselves with others, an act God considers unwise. As we engage in this unhealthy habit, we find that rather than focusing on finding our place in God's divine agenda, we indulge in an unnecessary competition that brings division. Other times, we find ourselves conforming to other people's opinions and ideas. For instance, if you grew up in an environment where words of affirmation were scarce and condemnation thrived, there is a likelihood that you might feel that you are not good enough. In some cases, you may even put others down just to feel better about yourself. Perhaps, because that is the lifestyle you are accustomed to, it'd be difficult to accept the truth of yourself until the Lord helps you. The Israelites had the same problem. They had endured so much hostility that they settled for a shadow of God's promises to them. They lost their sense of understanding God's divine purpose for them as a nation. Because they had no personal relationship with God, except one through their fathers who had died, they couldn't see beyond their circumstances.

After Joseph's death, a new King who did not know Joseph and his exploits in the Kingdom was enthroned. When He saw how fruitful the Israelites were in his land, he considered them a threat and gave instructions to the people to treat them harshly. He made the environment so unbearable for them, putting slave masters over them to oppress them. He said,

> Exodus 1:9-10 "Pharaoh said to his people, "Look, the people of Israel now outnumber us and are stronger than we are. We must make a plan to

keep them from growing even more. If we don't, and if war breaks out, they will join our enemies and fight against us. Then they will escape from the country." [NLT].

As a result, the Israelites lived in fear for many years. They forgot about God's promises and strived to survive by giving in to the pressing demands of the Egyptians. Despite the growing challenges, God still prospered them. Pharaoh saw this as a threat and ordered the murder of all newborn Hebrew boys. Killing the male children meant ending the lineage of the Israelites, the same lineage Jesus descended from. God disallowed his plans by causing the Hebrew women to find favor in the eyes of the Egyptian Midwives. When Pharaoh discovered this, he decided that a more effective strategy to achieve his goal was to resort to drowning the newborn boys. It was about the time Pharaoh put his plan into action that Jochebed became pregnant with Moses.

Moses, the young boy born in such a perilous time, was God's answer to the cry of the Israelites. Although he looked nothing like it in the beginning, he grew to become the deliverer of the Israelites, God's chosen people, and the one appointed by God to lead them into the land God had promised Canaan. He grew to become the greatest yet meekest leader the world has ever known. His life teaches us that God's divine purpose has little to do with our comfort or convenience and more to do with helping others experience His divine help. His divine purpose is greater than our personal goals, relationships, career, and even our ambitions. It had everything to do with His plan for His Kingdom and your role in fulfilling His purpose.

So, if you want to discover God's purpose for your life, the specific role you ought to play in His agenda, start in His presence. Seek to find out what your natural abilities are and how you can use them to dominate the Earth. Prioritizing our ambitions over His divine purpose will lead us into error. You were created to solve a problem. A generation is waiting for you to discover your assignment and become a solution. I'm sure Moses had his ambitions. If it were up to Him, he probably would have remained a shepherd in Midian. However, his desire to live beyond himself and fulfill God's purpose made him drop all his numerous excuses and trust God to lead Him right. Your life is in the hands of God. He holds your breath and gives it as he pleases. As long as you are alive, you have to discover your role in God's kingdom and work hard at fulfilling it. In the next chapter, I will be using the life of Moses to help you understand how God carefully directed Moses' path even up to the burning bush experience where he encountered God.

CHAPTER 2

THE PLIGHT OF A BASKET CASE

Jeremiah 1:5 *"I knew you before I formed you in your mother's womb. Before you were born I set you apart and appointed you as my prophet to the nations."* [**NLT**]

No matter where you are in your life right now, know this: God put you on this Earth to fulfill the purpose He has predestined for your life.

*— **Bishop T.D Jakes***

I n the previous chapter, we identified God's original intention for creating man (you and me). We were made to dominate the Earth using our God-given abilities, and the vast resources on the Earth to serve God and humanity. Because of Adam's disobedience, we lost the ability to commune with God directly and receive instructions for our lives and our assignment here on Earth. Jesus, the redemption plan of God, gave His life to restore us to do every good work God has predestined for us to do.

The story of Moses is an inspiration that shows how God can transform his life from the image he conformed to, into the man who led the Israelites across the Red Sea, down to the land God predestined for them. In this chapter, we will learn how God conceals His purposes and preserves His vessels, preparing and positioning them to fulfill His divine purpose. His story will teach you that God is committed to helping you discover and fulfill His purpose for your life.

Drawn out by faith - Moses' first draw

One day, while reading through Exodus 2, the first thing that caught my eyes was the season Moses was born. Moses was born at a perilous time, about the time when Pharaoh ordered the death of all newborn baby boys, including Moses. At that time, the Egyptians ruled over the Israelites. Seeing all the exploits done by Moses in the scriptures, I wonder why God chose to let the "Savior" of the Israelites be delivered into the world at such a time. I also realized that similar circumstances surrounded the birth of Jesus Christ. He was born at a time when the Romans ruled over the Israelites. When news of his birth reached Herod, Herod immediately ordered the execution of all the male children between the ages of 0-2 years old.

> Exodus 1:22 "Then Pharaoh gave this order to all his people: "Throw every newborn Hebrew boy into the Nile River. But you may let the girls live." [NLT].

> Matthew 2:16 "Herod was furious when he realized that the wise men had outwitted him. He sent soldiers to kill all the boys in and around Bethlehem who were two years old and under, based on the wise men's

report of the star's first appearance."
[NLT].

The first lesson to draw from the similarities in these scriptures is this: Whatever God has destined to do through you will be challenged by the enemy. Your assignment is such that it may attract both allies and enemies. For instance, David's exploits attracted Jonathan, the crown Prince of Israel. David, who was first a shepherd before he became a warrior, formed a close bond with Jonathan. The Bible recorded that Jonathan's heart cleaved to David.[3] If David refused to take the step and slay Goliath, he never would have experienced the true power of friendship. Jonathan did everything in his power to keep his father King Saul from killing King David. Faithful friends like Jonathan are rare, friends who see to it that you fulfill God's purpose for your life. Also, there will be people whose desire is to ensure you don't make it to fulfilling your assignment. Just like Pharaoh and Herod, their assignment will be to hinder you from getting to that point of discovering and fulfilling your purpose. If you observed the text above, you'd have noticed that it is the devil's sole responsibility

---

[3]   https://www.biblegateway.com/passage/?search=1+Samuel+18&version=NIV

to ensure none of God's plans for your life succeeds. Using the tool of distraction, he will go to any length to succeed in frustrating God's divine purpose for your life. I want you to know that for challenging situations, there is always wisdom to navigate through those challenges and emerge strong. James, one of the apostles of Jesus Christ, said;

> James 1:5, "If you need wisdom, ask our generous God, and he will give it to you. He will not rebuke you for asking." [NLT].

Jochebed received wisdom from God on how to preserve her son's life while Joseph and Mary also received specific instructions from God on how to keep Jesus from getting killed before His appointed time of death. They both were hidden for a while. To hide something means to keep away from prying eyes. Moses was kept hidden first in his birth home for 3 months then he was hidden in a basket with Miriam watching over him. Then, he was discovered, adopted, and then hidden in plain sight by Pharaoh's daughter. Hiding a newborn son for three months would have been extremely difficult for Jochebed and her family. Even more difficult was the tough decision regarding her son's future, leaving his life to chance on the Riverbank, with his little sister keeping watch. Anyone could have found Moses. He could have been discovered by one of the Egyptian guards and killed instantly. But God had great plans for Moses. His plan was so great that He ensured Moses got discovered by Pharaoh's daughter, in whose eyes he found favor. Moses was adopted by the princess, nursed by his mother, and raised in the palace of one who wanted him dead. Just some months before his delivery, His life was in great danger but God ensured His plans for Moses prevailed. He ensured Moses found safety in the lair of the enemy, using the princess to carry out His divine purpose.

One of God's strategies for our dominion here on Earth is by keeping things hidden until the appointed time. For instance, if the boys, Moses and Jesus were left in their place of abode at infancy, they would have been discovered and their destinies destroyed. They never would have gotten the chance to grow into maturity and fulfill God's divine purpose for their lives. The only person who knew everything about them was God, not their parents. Seeing the end from the beginning, he preserved them by first hiding them while he prepared them for His will. For the sake of His divine purpose, God can use anything or anyone to help you become what He has already predestined you to be. Had Moses been drowned in the Nile River, perhaps, the Israelites wouldn't have yet gained their freedom at that time. Perhaps, the coming of Jesus to redeem mankind would have been delayed. But God, in His infinite wisdom, turned an unfavorable situation into a glorious one.

Do you believe God has a plan for your life?

Just like Jesus and Moses, No one knows who you are. They can only try to form an opinion of your actions or your performance in a task at a given time. No one knows more about a product than the manufacturer. Some people live off the opinion of who we are and our social status. Sometimes, we let the media influence our thinking about ourselves. The truth is that no human being knows who you are better than the One who created you. The only one who knows you and can help you find meaning in your life is in you: The Holy Spirit. It takes faith for you to see how God uses unfavorable situations to prepare you to fulfill destiny. Jochebed, the mother of Moses, did not stop at believing. She followed her conviction and took a bold step of faith towards ensuring Moses' safety. Perhaps Amram and Jochebed saw that this child might be the one whom God would use to bring His promises to pass. Moses did bring about the promises of God in leading God's people out of slavery in Egypt. But Moses did not bring the final and ultimate rest promised to the people of God. No! He fulfilled His assignment. It took the birth of Jesus Christ to bring about the redemption of mankind. His parents believed and took steps of faith.

Cultivating faith in your heart is just what you need to discover and fulfill God's plan for your life. Moses' parents had good reasons to doubt and hold back in fear. Fear is a choice just as much as faith in God is a choice. In discovering your unique role in God's divine purpose, you must believe that God has great plans for you. Despite the challenges you are faced with, you need to trust God even in tough times. Trust that He has good plans for you. He has said in His word,

> Jeremiah 29:11 "For I know the plans
> I have for you," says the Lord. "They
> are plans for good and not for disaster,
> to give you a future and a hope."
> [NLT].

When you don't know what to do, remind yourself that God has great plans for you. Those times can be tough. We can either choose to let all kinds of thoughts flood our minds and distract us or we can open our hearts and let the Spirit of God have His way through prayers. Prayer has been proven to be a powerful tool that offers hope, comfort, and direction to those who engage its power. Through prayers, you are closer to God. Your mind is still, making it easy to recognize his voice. In the place of prayer, God gives direction. Here is how he said it in His Word,

> Jeremiah 29:12-13 "In those days when you pray, I will listen. If you look for me wholeheartedly, you will find me." [NLT].

> Isaiah 30:19-21 "O people of Zion, who live in Jerusalem, you will weep no more. He will be gracious if you ask for help. He will surely respond to the sound of your cries. Though the Lord gave you adversity for food and suffering for drink, he will still be with you to teach you. You will see your teacher with your own eyes. Your ears will hear him. Right behind you,

a voice will say, "This is the way you should go," whether to the right or the left." [NLT].

The best way to approach God is to come boldly, believing that He exists and He will give you an answer. Everyone used by God in the Holy Scriptures did not start out knowing their purpose in life. Yet, each one of them had one thing in common: they dared to believe God. Gideon, who considered himself to be the least in his family as well as his tribe chose to believe God's word and eventually became one of the best judges and a mighty warrior in Israel. How have you let your current circumstances and your past affect God's divine purpose for your life? Remember, regardless of the limitations you might have, God still desires to fulfill His divine purpose for you. Like Moses' mother responded to God's call, ensuring his safety, will you dare to believe and answer God's call on your life?

In the next chapter, we will be considering practical ways you can receive God's assignment for you and the specific instructions He will give to you on how to complete the assignment.

RECEIVING THE ASSIGNMENT AND INSTRUCTIONS

I Corinthians 7:17 *"But as God has distributed to each one, as the Lord has called each one, so let him walk. And so I ordain in all the churches."* [**NKJV**]

God will never advance your instructions beyond your last act of disobedience.

—Dr. Mike Murdock

One of the key lessons we learned in the previous chapter is that you need faith to discover and fulfill your assignment here on Earth. Without faith, it is impossible to build a conviction around His word and pursue His divine purpose. Your limitations and circumstances will keep interrupting your service to God. And as you know, you can't serve two masters. One will always be of a higher priority than the other. Prayer is an effective tool to discover God's specific assignment for you, including His instructions to guarantee your success.

One important secret about prayer is that it is a 2-way channel consisting of a transmitter and a receiver. With the transmitter, you talk to God, with the receiver, you listen to Him speak back to you. Speaking to God about your fears and desires to know His will for your life is one side of the coin. To have an encounter like Moses' burning bush experience, you need to know how to receive from God. Mike Murdock said, "you create a season of success every time you complete instruction from God." The instructions you hear from God while spending time in His presence will go a long way in transforming your life. In this chapter, I will use Moses' life as a template to confront five big fears we try to hide behind as we contemplate whether or not to accept the assignment.

Receiving the assignment – Moses' second draw

Moses' encounter with God in the field in Midian has always been an insightful study I particularly enjoy. The experiences that led up to Moses relocating to Midian was one of misplaced call of action. As a Prince of Egypt who walked into a fight between an Israelite and an Egyptian, Moses' response to the situation was quite unexpected. He killed the guard who was maltreating the Israelite. He tried to conceal what he had done. However, when he eventually got found out, he had to flee Midian where he became a shepherd and got married to Zipporah, Jethro's daughter.

40 years had passed and there was no call from God to Moses. It was as though God intentionally paid attention to how well he tended to the sheep before he decided to entrust Him with a bigger responsibility. Midian was like a place Moses played it safe. His decision to kill an Egyptian guard made him a target. Perhaps, Midian felt like it was the best place to unwind and hide from all his challenges.

Let me quickly interject at this point. Your past does not define your future. You should work on disallowing hurtful past experiences that affect your self-perception. Moses was not perfect yet God did not reject him. Rather, He thought he was a murderer yet God chose to use Moses to deliver His chosen people out of Israel. How often do you let past mistakes determine whether or not you are worthy of being used by God? You are more than your mistakes. God can still use you if you have made mistakes in the past. God is love and love keeps no memories of past misdeeds. So, do yourself a favor and stop dwelling in the past. Paul had a rough life. He persecuted the Christians and participated in the killing of Stephen, a man full of the spirit of wisdom. He may have had other bad experiences up to his sleeves but he did not let it define Him. Instead, He acknowledged God's sovereign power, responded to God's call, and submitted Himself to doing the works of ministry. In one of His letters, he said,

> Philippians 3:12-14 I don't mean to say that I have already achieved these things or that I have already reached perfection. But I press on to possess that perfection for which Christ Jesus

first possessed me. No, dear brothers and sisters, I have not achieved it, but I focus on this one thing: Forgetting the past and looking forward to what lies ahead, I press on to reach the end of the race and receive the heavenly prize for which God, through Christ Jesus, is calling us. [NLT].

You were created to solve a specific problem God saw on the Earth. Every day, people send prayers up to heaven asking God to intervene in those situations. God cannot come down from heaven to meet those needs. He uses willing vessels to achieve His purposes. The Israelites endured suffering from their Egyptian masters. Their cries for help moved God's heart to help them. To deliver His people, God needed a man, one with a willing heart prepared to answer the call. So, he said to Moses,

Exodus 3:7-10 Then the Lord told him, "I have certainly seen the oppression of my people in Egypt. I have heard their cries of distress because of their harsh slave drivers. Yes, I am aware of their suffering. **So I have come down to rescue them from the power of the Egyptians and lead them out of Egypt into their own fertile and spacious land.** It is a land flowing with milk and honey—the land where the Canaanites, Hittites, Amorites, Perizzites, Hivites, and Jebusites now live. Look! The cry of the people of Israel has reached me, and I have seen how harshly the Egyptians abuse them. Now go, for I am sending you to Pharaoh. **You must lead my people Israel out of Egypt.**" [NLT]

If you pay careful attention to the bolded part of the above text, you will notice that God was the one going to deliver His people but he needed Moses to be the Earthly vessel he would work with in partnership to deliver the Israelites. The Holy Spirit was given to us for the same reason - to work in partnership with us to fulfill our earthly assignment. He is God in us, working in us to do the good works God predestined for us before time. Unfortunately, many times, we neglect Him, trying hard to accomplish things on our own. Sometimes, we let our limitations cloud our judgment so much that we do not give Him room to help us. Moses did the same thing with God. He focused more on what he did not have than what He already had but didn't realize. I will be sharing with you five excuses we give that can limit us from receiving the assignment. You should pick the one that applies most to you and see the provision God has made for every one of those inadequacies.

Five excuses that hinder us from receiving the assignment

1. *I honestly don't think I am good enough to lead*

Exodus 3:11 But Moses protested to God, "Who am I to appear before Pharaoh? Who am I to lead the people of Israel out of Egypt?" [NLT].

When God calls us to begin an assignment, one of the traps we fall into is the one that reads, "Hello Lord! I'm not enough to complete this task..." We focus more on our talents, gifts, abilities, and resources, forgetting that He who has called us is faithful. Usually, when God says, "Go do this for me." He already knows your limitations. He knows you have weaknesses which are why He never sends you alone. Moses had been in

Midian tending sheep for a while. His past and perhaps his environment affected His perception so much that He had no more confidence in his abilities anymore. The only problem with Moses' response was this: Not only had he lost confidence in his abilities. He had no recollection of God's unlimited power to help him. He couldn't see through the eyes of faith rather he focused more on the facts of his circumstances. And God said,

> Exodus 3:12 "I will be with you. And this is your sign that I am the one who has sent you: When you have brought the people out of Egypt, you will worship God at this very mountain." [NLT].

God's presence is one of the greatest assets we can have when embarking on an assignment. He put His Spirit in us so that we can have unlimited access to Him, any day, any time, anywhere. What this means is that we can always count on God to help guide us through the assignment, saving ourselves from unnecessary mistakes rather than lean on our understanding.

2. *I have insufficient knowledge*

Exodus 3:13 NLT But Moses protested, "If I go to the people of Israel and tell them, "The God of your ancestors has sent me to you," they will ask me, "What is his name?" Then what should I tell them?" [NLT].

Like Moses, we are sometimes scared of our inadequacies, forgetting that the One who has sent us is All-knowing. His Spirit, the spirit of truth, dwells in us and He can help bring to our remembrance whatever we need to know. If only we knew and maximize the full benefits of having the Spirit of God dwelling in us. The truth is this: we can never know enough. Neither are we going to be completely ready. If this were possible then we wouldn't need God's strength to cover for our weaknesses. You don't have to know everything in the beginning. He teaches you and guides you as you go. Like He said to Moses, He is saying to you,

> Exodus 3:14 " I Am Who I Am. Say
> this to the people of Israel: I Am has
> sent me to you." [NLT].

The name "I AM" connotes limitless possibilities. So, this means that what you do not know, you only need to ask Him for wisdom and He'd teach you more, beyond what any book can teach you. He prepares you and equips you along the way. It's just like the popular saying that goes, God does not call the equipped. He equips the called."

3. *I am afraid I may fail*

Exodus 4:1 But Moses protested again, "What if they won't believe me or listen to me? What if they say, "The Lord never appeared to you"?" [NLT].

Have you observed that fear of failure kills dreams, visions, and divine assignments faster than failure itself? It keeps us stuck in self-dilemma as we assess all the possible reasons why we think we cannot succeed at it. Most of the things we imagine never end up happening most of the time, yet, it is difficult to convince someone that they can succeed at anything if you quit overanalyzing things before you do them. It is good to consider the possibility of encountering challenges along the way. However, it is wrong to let it keep you in a state of inertia. God promised to provide for Moses' assignment, using what was in his hands (his staff). Paraphrased, here is what he said in response to Moses' excuse in Exodus 4:2-9. He said,

"You don't have to worry about the plan failing. I will be with you every step of the way, providing everything you need. All you have to do is trust me."

God is saying this to you today. You don't have to worry about whether or not the plan will work out. As long as it is a God-given assignment, He will provide all you need.

4. *I have a few weaknesses*

Exodus 4:10 But Moses pleaded with the Lord, "O Lord, I'm not very good with words. I never have been, and I'm not now, even though you have spoken to me. I get tongue-tied, and my words get tangled." [NLT].

Moses had a speech impediment. As such, he felt he was unqualified to lead a nation. What limitation do you have that is hindering you from receiving your assignment? Do you think you are too short? Or too tall? Or too skinny? Or too loud? God created you that way for a reason. He is not oblivious to any limitation you might think that you have. There are two ways I saw God respond to this kind of limitation that helped me in my Christian journey. First, in response to Moses' complaint, he said

> Exodus 4:11 Then the Lord asked Moses, "Who makes a person's mouth? Who decides whether people speak or do not speak, hear, or do not hear, see, or do not see? Is it not I, the Lord? Now go! I will be with you as you speak, and I will instruct you in what to say." [NLT].

When God calls you, what he looks for **first** is your willingness, not your skillfulness. He seeks for one who desires to do His will and grow in the process. Through His mighty power at work in us, He can do anything, including covering our weakness with His strength. Paul, as great as he was, had some struggles along the way. He cried to God about it, asking Him to take it away. Here is what God said,

> 2 Corinthians 12:7-10 "Even though I have received such wonderful revelations from God. So to keep me from becoming proud, I was given

a thorn in my flesh, a messenger from Satan to torment me and keep me from becoming proud. Three different times I begged the Lord to take it away. Each time he said, "My grace is all you need. My power works best in weakness." So now I am glad to boast about my weaknesses so that the power of Christ can work through me. That's why I take pleasure in my weaknesses, and in the insults, hardships, persecutions, and troubles that I suffer for Christ. For when I am weak, then I am strong." [NLT].

The disciples whom Jesus Christ equipped were not skillful at first. They just had the willingness. As they progressed in their walk with Jesus, they grew and became more deeply grounded. Whenever you remember your frailties, commit them to God and depend on His Grace. His Grace is sufficient. It is in your weakness that His strength will be seen and He gets the glory for helping you with his limitless power.

5. *I'm unavailable*

Exodus 4:13 But Moses again pleaded, "Lord, please! Send anyone else." [NLT].

A lack of willingness to accept the assignment even after seeing God's desire to provide all we need for success grieves God. In the subsequent verse, God expressed His displeasure at Moses' inability to trust Him and move past the limiting strongholds in His mind. He desires that we trust Him to see us through the process. In Moses' case, he decided to introduce a person who'd assist Moses in carrying out the assignment. He introduced Aaron, Moses' brother, to be his spokesman, working as a team to fulfill His assignment.

With God, you are never stranded. No matter how much you think your limitations are, God has something better in store for you. He has a solution that will require your trust and complete dependence on Him. When God asks you to begin an assignment, no matter how valid your excuses are, I want you to know that it will work. Why? It is because you will be teaming up with the most powerful source on Earth, the Holy Spirit, and other quality relationships He will bring your way. Remember: to receive the assignment and accompanying instructions, you must have an open heart. You must also believe in God's ability to help you. Most importantly, you must remember that He created you just the way you are. So, you are perfect for your assignment.

I'd like to challenge you to take a step of faith this week. What has God laid in your heart to do that you may have ignored? Do you commit to confronting those fears you have and don't hold back? Trust in him with all your heart and lean wholly only on Him. Acknowledge Him in everything you do. After all, it's His assignment and He will surely be there to guide you every step of the way.

CHAPTER 4

NAVIGATING THROUGH YOUR DIVINE PURPOSE

One of the most fascinating things I discovered while studying the life of Moses is how much he grew. From being a timid and angry man, Moses grew to become one of the exemplary leaders in history today. From being one full of excuses, Moses embraced and fulfilled God's purpose for his life. I do not think there is a record stating that his stutter was cured. Yet, he led the Israelites for over 40 years.

One of the secret strategies I discovered from the life of Moses that helped him navigate through His divine purpose was this: He valued god's presence

Exodus 33:15-16 Then Moses said, "If you don't personally go with us, don't make us leave this place. How will anyone know that you look favorably on me—on me and your people—if you don't go with us? For your presence among us sets your people and me apart from all other people on the earth." [NLT].

All through scriptures, men who made any progress in fulfilling God's divine purpose had just one prayer on their lips, "Lord if your presence does not go with me, I cannot go." Great men like David, Joseph, and even Moses in Exodus 33, made this kind of intimate prayer. Isn't it surprising to see Moses' name on the list of those crying out for God's presence considering he did not want to go before Pharaoh with God's presence only? Having gone through the series of training and pruning, Moses was transformed into who God destined Him to be. He grew to understand that without God's presence, there is no fulfillment of His divine purpose. As a believer seeking to fulfill your purpose, you must prioritize the Holy Spirit above all else. The primary role the Holy Spirit plays in your life is to reveal the truth about ourselves to us. As we progress in life, there will be too many voices trying to pull your attention.

However, being intimate with God makes it easy for you to recognize God's instructions, distinguishing it from man's opinions. Knowing the Holy Spirit's voice, especially how He speaks to you, makes it easy for you to understand God's divine purpose at every season in your life.

Another strategy that helped Moses navigate through purpose was intimacy with God. His progressive understanding of God's nature and principles helped him to become an excellent leader. He honored God despite his close relationship with Him. He also played the role of an intercessor, just like Jesus Christ, especially when the Israelites offended God with their thirst for idol worship. Also, Moses built confidence in the leadership process. Every experience in the wilderness was an opportunity to grow into a better leader. Because of his unrelenting commitment to carry out God's purpose, his life serves as a lesson for all of us pressing towards the mark.

In closing, I'd like to encourage you to spend time discovering and preparing for your purpose. Do not let anything, anyone, or any experience define you. If you stay focused and fix your eyes on Jesus, you will finish strong. The Holy Spirit is the only one who can point you in the right direction. He is the Spirit that has access to the intents of the Father concerning your life. This verse perfectly sums it up:

1 Corinthians 2:7-16 But it was to us that God revealed these things by his Spirit. For His Spirit searches out everything and shows us God's deep secrets. No one can know a person's thoughts except that person's spirit, and no one can know God's thoughts except God's own Spirit. And we have received God's Spirit (not the world's spirit), so we can know the wonderful things God has freely given us. When we tell you these things, we do not use words that come from human wisdom. Instead, we speak words given to us by the Spirit, using the Spirit's words to explain spiritual truths. But people who aren't spiritual can't receive these truths from God's Spirit. It all sounds foolish to them and they can't understand it, for only those who are spiritual can understand what the Spirit means. Those who are spiritual can evaluate all things, but they cannot be evaluated by others. For, "Who can know the Lord 's thoughts? Who knows enough to teach him?" But we understand these things, for we have the mind of Christ. [NLT].

The Holy Spirit lives in you. Therefore, you are wired to do exploits. You should embrace God's divine purpose for your life and watch Him transform you as he did with Moses.

SUMMARY

I t is great to see that you made it to the end of this book. I have summarized this book, highlighting key points that will help you as you journey through life.

- Purpose is the reason why a being was created or a thing exists. It answers the question, *"Why am I here?"*

- God's Divine Purpose for your life is simply His reason for creating you, endowing you with the special abilities you have, and strategically placing you here on Earth.

- We were made to dominate the Earth using our God-given abilities, and the vast resources on the Earth to serve God and humanity.

- To restore Man to his original intention for creation, God sent His son Jesus Christ to pay the ultimate price for our redemption. His goal was to restore our communion with God, restore us to His image, and restore dominion over the domain (Earth) He gave us complete authority over.

- So, if you want to discover God's purpose for your life, the specific role you ought to play in His agenda, start in His presence.

- Seek to find out what your natural abilities are and how you can use them to dominate the Earth.

- You were created to solve a problem. A generation is waiting for you to discover your assignment and become a solution.

- Whatever God has destined to do through you will be challenged by the enemy. Your assignment is such that it may attract both allies and enemies.

- One of God's strategies for our dominion here on Earth is by keeping things hidden until the appointed time. Here, he prepares them for the assignment.

- Cultivating faith in your heart is just what you need to discover and fulfill God's plan for your life.

- When you don't know what to do, remind yourself that God has great plans for you. Those times can be tough. We can either choose to let all kinds of thoughts flood our minds and distract us or we can open our hearts and let the Spirit of God have His way through prayers.

- You need faith to discover and fulfill your assignment here on Earth. Without faith, it is impossible to build a conviction around His word and pursue His divine purpose. Your limitations and circumstances will keep interrupting your service to God.

- Your past does not define your future. You should work on disallowing hurtful past experiences that affect your self-perception.

- Through prayers, you are closer to God. Your mind is still, making it easy to recognize his voice.

- The best way to approach God is to come boldly, believing that He exists and He will give you an answer.

- Everyone used by God in the Holy Scriptures did not start out knowing their purpose in life. Yet, each one of them had one thing in common: they dared to believe God.

- Every day, people send prayers up to heaven asking God to intervene in those situations. God cannot come down from heaven to meet those needs. He uses willing vessels to achieve His purposes.

- God's presence is one of the greatest assets we can have when embarking on an assignment. He put His Spirit in us so that we can have unlimited access to Him, any day, any time, anywhere.

- We can never know enough. Neither are we going to be completely ready. If this were possible then we wouldn't need God's strength to cover for our weaknesses. You don't have to know everything in the beginning. He teaches you and guides you as you go.

- You don't have to worry about whether or not the plan will work out. As long as it is a God-given assignment, He will provide all you need.

- When God calls you, what he looks for **first** is your willingness, not your skillfulness. He seeks for one who desires to do His will and grow in the process.

- With God, you are never stranded. No matter how much you think your limitations are,

God has something better in store for you. He has a solution that will require your trust and complete dependence on Him.

- As a believer seeking to fulfill God's purpose for your life, you must prioritize your relationship with the Holy Spirit above all else. The primary role the Holy Spirit plays in your life is to reveal the truth about ourselves to us.

ABOUT THE AUTHOR

Samuel Duncan, IV is a native of Lansing, MI. He currently serves as Assistant Pastor to his father. With a heart to help people discover their God ordained purpose in life, Samuel inspires through his preaching, consulting, coaching, and leadership development.

www.ingramcontent.com/pod-product-compliance
Lightning Source LLC
Chambersburg PA
CBHW070542080426
42453CB00029B/985